Essays From God's Country

Essays From God's Country

by

LEE PITTS

Cover Painting, Running With The Mares by Tim Cox

First Edition

Inquiries regarding this book should be addressed to:
Lee Pitts
P.O. Box 616
Morro Bay, CA 93443

Cover painting by Tim Cox
Printed by Image Graphics, Paducah, KY

International Standard Book Number 0-9666334-2-3

CONTENTS

CONTENTS

I think we could use a little more country in this country. I believe this country needs less cultivation and more cultivation, if you know what I mean? More concern about sowing than reaping.

Country residents know they get the most important news from their neighbors, not CNN. They get their stock quotes in prices per pound, not scandals per company.

People who live in the country know that being stalled in the fast lane is no way to spend a life. They are not bored by their own company or enslaved by a clock. They know that a bad book is better than the best TV, and that entertainment can be provided by a firefly.

Lightly peopled places give children a place to crash land or fall to the ground safely when spreading their wings. Residents of the country don't want it all and realized long ago that all they have is all they need.

Country folks are a more patient people. They plant seeds and water them with optimism and faith, for they realize that good things take time. And care. Rural residents like to say they live in "God's Country" and simple pleasures remind them on a daily basis that they do.

This book is dedicated to all those who live in God's Country.

HAND-ME-DOWN DREAMS

THE BEST THING that parents can give a child is a brother or sister. The loneliest sounding words in our language are "only child." No child should have to invent an imaginary friend when they could have the real thing. Happiness really is a relative, and the more the better.

Not that siblings don't have their issues. Little brothers and sisters have been known to tattle-tale, mess with your toys and humiliate you in front of friends when you are forced to take them with you. And can there be anything worse than having to sit through a little sister's dance recital or first violin concert? Other than being forced to go to the prom with your brother, of course.

With siblings there are constant territorial battles over the limited real estate in the family car, a shared bedroom or mommy's lap. One has to fight for control of the TV remote and daddy's limited attention span. Arguments never cease over whose turn it is to take out the trash, to mow or to clip, to wash or to wipe. Is there anyone more thoughtless than an older brother or sister who fails to consider your taste in clothes when picking out theirs, knowing you will one day inherit their hand-me-downs?

Allowances may be smaller when divided more ways but at least there's someone to share the work. And the blame. You may receive more Christmas presents as an only child but there is no one to share them with. Besides, gifts that belonged to a sibling were more fun to play with than your own toys anyway. The best thing about brothers and sisters is your parents can hardly keep you from playing with them, even if they are the kind of kids they told you not to associate with.

Sisters have more than genes and jeans in common, they also share makeup, shoes, secrets and boyfriends. Whether they knew it or not at the time. Brothers share baseball bats, bedrooms and bath water. I swear I didn't know the feel of hot water till my brother left home. Although, in all honesty, I'd gladly go back to cold bath water if I could just see my brother more.

It's often thought that the first child is favored because parents, being new at the job, are more careful in their parenting. "Mom always liked you best," is a common complaint. But parents don't pick favorites, they just love their children differently. So what if the first born is a genius or a perfect child in mom's or dad's eyes? They also serve a purpose. They blaze a trail and set a standard for how much good grades are worth or the going rate from the tooth fairy. They scout out the best teachers and usher parents through their overprotective stage, allowing younger sibs to forgo all the humiliation that can entail.

That doesn't mean brotherhood and sisterhood is easy. In school you are immediately recognized as so-and-so's kin. It's probably the hand-me-down clothes the teacher recognized. It is exciting to discover a book with your sister's name in it or a desk with your brother's initials carved in the wood. Then reality sets in. Either your siblings made a favorable impression you can't live up to, or a reputation you can't live down.

Parents are fine as far as they go, but brothers and sisters do the real dirty work in raising a family. Screening dates for little sister or beating back bullies who pester a younger brother. They teach the really important stuff too, like how to throw a curve ball or a slumber party. When you have a brother or sister you will always have someone to talk to, confide in and cover for you because they can't resign, quit or relinquish the job. Whether it's your dog that dies or one of your folks, it's probably the hand of a sibling that will find its way to yours. They provide brotherly love and sisterly compassion like only they can. At their best a brother or sister can inspire imitation, foster feelings of family, and hand down their dresses, their duds and their dreams.

A Mixed Marriage

THOSE OF YOU who have never had the misfortune of meeting me may not realize that I'm part of a "mixed marriage." That's right, my wife is a night person and I'm a morning person. You may scoff at the distinction and think it slight, but I happen to think it's a very BIG difference. Even bigger than a Capricorn and a Libra hooking up, a Democrat and a Republican or a Catholic and a Protestant. Those differences can be overcome with good counseling and therapy. But not the AM/PM thing.

I love mornings and try to do everything important in the early hours just in case something goes wrong, then I haven't wasted the whole day. Take our marriage for example. The morning after our wedding I got up and approached my new bride's side of the bed, gazed down on her sweet face and sang in a lilting voice, "Wake up, wake up you sleepyhead. Come on, come on get out of bed." She opened one eye, snarled and growled, "If you ever wake me up this early again I swear it will be the last time." And it was nine-thirty in the morning!

A couple days later after she had cooled off I made the mistake of simply saying, "Good morning."

She got that look in her eye again and grumbled, "There's no such thing."

"But don't you remember," I replied, "I asked you what time you liked to get up in the morning before I even proposed marriage. And you said you got up as soon as the first ray of sunlight came through your window."

"That's right," she agreed. "But don't you also remember that it was summer at the time and my room faced west. You knew I was a night person. Do you really think I'd have consented to marrying you if I ever got a good look at you in the daylight?"

I had to admit she had a good point there. So, now I stay up until all hours of the night waiting for her to come home. Please, don't misunderstand. My wife works a lot of night shifts. Many evenings she doesn't get off till ten or eleven when most normal people have already had half a good night's sleep. No, my wife's not lazy, in fact she can outwork any three men and often does. It's just that her biological clock is wound different than mine. I often fall asleep right in my early bird supper whereas she has actually seen the eleven o'clock news on TV. I turn into a sleeping bag at eight and she hasn't even had lunch by then.

Being married to a night person is difficult, as I'm sure many of you men can attest. You can't even talk to a morning wife until after ten and by then half the day is gone. My wife is like a car that's hard to start in the morning but once you get her started you can't turn her off. This was evident recently when we went to a dinner party. I usually don't get invited to many of these type of events because the hosts mistake my yawning for rudeness and boredom. As usual my wife and I had a prearranged agreement that when I made a certain sign it was time to go home. So, about 8:30 I caught her eye figuring if we left then I could be home and in bed by nine. Later than usual, I'll admit, but once in a while I let my hair down and go crazy.

I gave my wife the sign and she ignored me, pretending not to even see me. In fact, she ignored me till 1:30 in the morning! By then I was ready to get up. "What's for breakfast?" I asked when we got in the car to go home.

Despite the fact that my wife is a night person and I'm a morning person we have worked out an arrangement that has enabled us to enjoy over a quarter-century of wedded bliss. She doesn't wake me up when I fall asleep in the recliner during the six o' clock news and I continue to let her work nights. What kind of a nice guy am I? Oh, and one more thing I credit for our long and happy marriage: one night a week without fail we go someplace. I go to bed. I have no idea where she goes.

IN REMEMBRANCE

IN SMALL TOWNS across this country weekly newspapers are carrying obituaries like these on a far too regular basis. I'm sure you can put a face to these fine folks.

Small Business Owner: Mr. and Mrs. Small Business Owner passed on recently after a lengthy stay in Intensive Care. The lifelong community residents had operated the local drug store for 37 years before shutting its doors after a short but terminal battle with Big Box Stores. An autopsy was performed and the cause of death was diagnosed as "Lower Prices and Bigger Selection."

The family had been popular members of the community having sponsored numerous Little League teams, YMCA, Girl Scouts and anyone else who came calling. Many residents will remember the wife as an active volunteer at the local hospital and hospice. The husband was active in the Elks Club and VFW. Together Mr. and Mrs. Small Business Owner enjoyed their active participation in the Chamber of Commerce and were a permanent fixture at local high school football games.

They are survived by a multinational conglomerate who promises to offer a wider variety and selection from sweatshops around the world. The Small Business Owners will hardly be remembered by their many "loyal" friends and customers who stopped shopping at their store the minute a Big Box Grand Opening was held. No services are planned and in lieu of flowers contributions should be sent directly to corporate headquarters in a big city far away.

Family Farmer and Rancher: Having carried on a family tradition on the same ground for three generations the Family Farmer and Rancher recently departed our community. Precipitating their exodus were low commodity prices, bungling bureaucrats and a society that couldn't care less.

Favorite family pastimes for the long married couple included gardening, quilting, helping friends and neighbors at brandings and making things out of nothing. They also enjoyed fishing and hunting together before that became widely scorned by society. The family was well-known for their intense love of the land and they were active members in the community. She taught Sunday School and he was active in the local Soil Conservation District, Farm Bureau and the Rotary Club. They leave behind many friends and neighbors who are in the same boat. They are survived by five kids, 15 grandchildren and 26 great grandchildren, none of whom want to step foot ever again on a farm or a ranch.

A quiet observance for family members was held as the rental truck hauled away their possessions along with a lifetime of memories.

No burial is planned as they are aren't dead yet. They merely moved to town where it just feels like it.

The Traditional Family: After extended exposure to an epidemic of greed, self-fulfillment and bad parenting, the Family Unit left us quietly without great fanfare. The Family's parting was precipitated by divorce, day care, and disregard. Its death was hastened by parents who talked to their stockbroker more than their kids and frequently went from matrimony to alimony in three short years. Henceforth, children will be raised by gangs, prisons, Internet chat rooms and the global village.

The Family leaves behind countless sons and daughters without any idea of the joy of family life. No one will be in charge of funeral arrangements because nobody seems to care. Contributions could have been made to a church but the family no longer had the time to belong to one.

The Community: Abandoned and abused, the small rural community passed away after a long illness. Few family members or friends were present at the end. Pallbearers included two bankers, an equipment dealer, the pastor and the editor of the weekly newspaper. They carried the Community while it was alive so it was fitting that they finished the job. The Community was preceded in passing by the death of the Small Businessman, the Family Farmer and Rancher and the Traditional Family Unit.

AIN'T NUTHIN' BUT A POUND DOG

I HAVE BOTTLE fed a litter of baby rabbits, applied a splint to a fawn's broken leg and helped save a hummingbird from a snare of cobwebs. I won't go out of my way to squash even the most heinous of bugs and I throw back any fish I don't intend to eat. We even turn the house lights off at night when the kamikaze moths attempt to commit suicide by flying through our plate glass window. I spent days giving IV's to a cat I never liked and when it got well it still treated me with catty contempt and attempted to scratch my eyes out.

And yet, the animal rightists say I am evil.

The other day my wife brought me my toughest case yet as an amateur animal surgeon. A homeless lizard had been trying to set up housekeeping in a cardboard box and in the process had become permanently affixed to the carton by some tacky tape. Considering the delicate condition of the lizard it was indeed a "sticky" situation. Using a set of tweezers I got one lizard leg free but then its tail got stuck. I am proud to say that after twenty minutes I was able to remove the lizard with all its appendages in place and the recovered reptile has thanked me every day since by taking up residence by our front door and scaring away those who peddle religion and assorted merchandise door-to-door.

And animal rights groups call me a criminal because I cultivate cows!

I am not alone in my concern for members of the animal kingdom. I have seen a macho cowboy bawl his eyes out over the death of his dog. And I know from experience that losing a horse is like losing a member of the family. We love animals... that's why we raise them.

I can only remember one time in my life when I did a really cruel thing to an animal and the episode haunts me to this day. I was mowing the lawn when I noticed a forlorn looking dog looking lost. By playing hard to get I was able to lure the dog into my shop and close the door. He must have been running a long time because the thirsty pooch lapped up three bowls of water before falling asleep at my feet. We got along famously but I knew I could not keep the dog because it was wearing a bright and shiny new collar with tags.

I called the county animal shelter and had to listen to a tape describing all the dead pets that had been delivered DOA. After playing phone tag for twenty minutes I was able to actually speak to a real person and give her the tag number of the lost dog. Computers can be wonderful! Within seconds I was told the dog had recently been adopted from the pound and its new name was Reginald.

That should have been my first clue. No one who truly loved animals would name a dog Reginald. I should have just "lost" the tags and kept the dog.

As if in a kidnapping movie the delivery was arranged, without a ransom, of course. A very excited lady arrived at the scene and said she was "Reggie's mother." I expected gratitude but got only grief. It seems that Reggie's mother was an animal rightist and she didn't approve of my keeping cows.

The reunion was pitiful. Reggie's mom dropped to one knee and began babbling baby talk. "Oh puppsy wuppsy where has my doggy woggy been? I love you so muchy much." As the pound dog was being pummeled with kisses he looked at me with sad eyes as if to say, "How could you do this to me? I had escaped."

Returning that dog was the cruelest thing I have ever done to an animal.

GOD'S COUNTRY

I THINK WE could use a little more country in this country. No, I'm not talking about adding some real estate: I'm talking about an attitude. Even if we all can't live in the country we can adopt some of the ways of our "countrymen."

Country residents know they get the most important news from their neighbors, not CNN. They get their stock quotes in prices per pound, not scandals per company. In the country people know that if the weather man calls for rain on the weekend it is cause to rejoice, not an excuse to mope around the house. Country folks know that being a good neighbor is far more important than keeping up with the Joneses. And if a fence needs mending both sides should work to fix it.

Oh sure, rural roads are more dusty but they're also a lot less crowded. People who live in the country know that being stalled in the fast lane for hours on end every day is no way to spend a life. They are more apt to give you a wave than the middle digit of a stressed out hand. About the only time you see bumper to bumper traffic in the country is for a funeral procession and most everyone for miles around knows who's in the box. Those that don't take off their hats anyway because they know that every life is worthy of respect.

Lightly peopled places give children a place to crash land or fall to the ground safely when spreading their wings. Residents of the country don't want it all and realized long ago that all they have is all they need. Their day is not ruined by a bad wine list, a snippy store clerk or by things that don't concern them. They eat their own cooking, play the hand that's dealt them and don't feel victimized when things go bad.

I believe this country needs less cultivation and more cultivation, if you know what I mean? More concern about sowing than reaping. Our fellow countrymen believe in fewer subdivisions and exclusive country clubs and more potlucks. They know that people are often divided by geography but that should be about all.

You may call them hicks or rubes but natives of the countryside like things more familiar and less foreign. They tend to be people who stay put instead of looking around for new places to mess up. Their air is not filled with the smoggy sounds of trains, planes and cars, of people going somewhere else, because they're satisfied right where they are. The natives are not naive, they know there's a big world out there, but they also know there's a better one right in their own backyard yet to be discovered.

Country citizens are worried less about the global economy than they are the local one. I like to think they are probably more honest because there's nowhere to hide: No glass and concrete skyscrapers to hide in or behind. They have to look their neighbors, friends and investors in the eye on a regular basis. And when they say, "Thanks," they try to mean it. They are also more self-sufficient, they make do with what they have because they can't run to the store every time they run out of milk.

Out in the boonies folks know that daylight is for working and playing and dark is for sleeping. They're not bored by their own company or enslaved by a clock. They know a bad book is better than the best TV, and that entertainment can be provided by a firefly. They know that nature is not a separate species and our wildlife is not endangered, but common sense is. They believe that people should have more rights than rocks and private property always looks better than non-resident owned. They honor the Motherland and the Fatherland and believe each home should have one of each... one father and one mother.

Country folks are a more patient people. They plant seeds and water them with optimism and faith for they realize that good things take time. And care. Residents of the countryside like to say they live in "God's Country," and simple pleasures remind them on a daily basis that they do.

THE HYPOCRITIC OATH

I SWEAR AN OATH on my honor as a hypocrite that...

I will cuss cows but eat beef, blast miners but wear jewelry and drive a car but condemn oil companies. I don't want trees cut for any purpose other than to provide the lumber for my next house.

As a Hollywood celebrity I assert my God given right to sire at least four children by three different wives and then protest about overpopulation in the world.

I will put fish first by saving the sucker and salmon, but not the farmers and ranchers who feed me. I demand that politicians and federal judges in Washington DC save all endangered species, except the small business man. I feel government is imminently qualified to micromanage nature, after all, look what a smashing job they've done with the IRS, EPA, USDA, FBI, BLM and assorted other alphabet agencies.

As a self righteous hypocrite it is my duty to celebrate Earth Day with barbecues and parades and by leaving tons of trash behind. I demand that feedlots and farms stop polluting our ground water. That privilege should be preserved for me every time I flush the contents of my toilet into a septic tank or the ocean.

I want to relocate grizzly bears and wolves to the West but not in my big city backyard. After all, people live here! I give my permission for mountain lions to eat lambs but if a lion eats my dog or cat I demand the abominable beast be shot on sight.

I will cuss oil companies on talk radio and stand in the way of them drilling more wells while sitting in my gas guzzling SUV with the engine running. I will write letters to the editor on my computer castigating utility companies for not providing enough electricity. At the same time I will send money to green groups who want to tear down hydroelectric dams and stand in the way of any new power producing projects.

I avow at the next cocktail party I attend while smoking a cigarette and sipping a martini that I will sue the tobacco companies for causing my lung cancer.

Although I have never personally milked a cow or grown vegetables in a garden I demand to have a say on how farmers and ranchers do it. As a pompous hypocrite I demand that water, herbicides and pesticides be taken away from farmers immediately, but I don't want it to effect the price, quantity or quality of the food I buy in the store. It is my strongly held conviction that we should ban all pesticides, except the can of bug spray I use to kill ants and other unwanted bugs in my home.

As a mealy-mouthed hypocrite I vow to help stop global warming by watching the Discovery Channel on my giant sized television in my air conditioned house.

I assert that cattle pooping on our nation's grasslands is a national disgrace while fertilizing my urban lawn with steer manure and urea is simply good ecology. I will complain about fertilizer runoff from farms but not from golf courses because I happen to be a golfer.

I will hound hunters in the woods because they use guns despite the fact that hunting groups have increased habitat and wildlife numbers. I demand that the government end all timber cutting in our national forests but I'll cry like a singed coyote if the feds allow wildfires to burn near my house.

As a card carrying hypocrite I disavow the use of fur, leather, wool and all animal by-products, except the ones used in medicine that might save my life. I demand labels be placed on all food products but not on a rock album that endorses killing cops.

Finally, as an arrogant and self-serving hypocrite I firmly believe that rural folks have done a terrible job of taking care of the countryside and they must do a better job because that's where I want to live or visit some day when I can escape the pollution, crime, and insanity of the barren big city in which I currently reside.

POTLUCK

I HAVEN'T BEEN to a good old fashioned church supper since several members of the congregation had to have their stomachs pumped when the luck ran out of the potluck.

Do they still have potluck suppers? No, I'm not referring to modern day dinner parties where a busy career woman picks up something from the deli or the bakery. Or cooks up a dish whose entire recipe reads: Thaw.

When I was a kid our church held a potluck every month. They were glorious affairs and every family would bring a casserole, dessert, or peas, along with their own silverware and plates. The only thing our church provided was the coffee, cooked in a vessel the size of a dipping vat. It was some of the best food I ever ate.

For the women of the church these were serious competitions. A potluck dinner was no place to try out a new, unproven recipe and many of the dishes had been handed down from one generation to the next. My mother always cooked up her scrumptious lasagna which was so good other Sunday School kids were actually envious of me. They thought we ate that way every night at my house. Other favorites I vividly recall were green beans and bacon, scalloped potatoes with ham and a tamale pie that was better than any whipped cream or fruit pie I've ever tasted.

Young potlicking potluckers, like myself, knew the contributors only by their specialty. It was a sad day indeed when "the Chocolate Cake Lady" switched churches due to a simple misunderstanding regarding top billing in the church newsletter. The informal winner of the competition was whoever's dish disappeared the fastest and the results decided the pecking order of the church social scene.

There was only one land mine to navigate at the church potluck and that was uncovering the dish brought by the one non-cook in the crowd. Delphine insisted on bringing a concoction that was either a thick soup or a thin Jello®. It tasted like potpourri and smelled like fish bait.

Suffering from a lack of edible nourishment, Delphine's family never missed a potluck supper. We only had to eat her food once a month but they had to eat it on a regular basis. We felt so sorry for Delphine's family the preacher never failed to say a prayer for their good health. The family was so malnourished they all had to stand in one place to cast a shadow. They were under Doctor's orders to eat out more often.

Despite subtle hints that Delphine should just pick up a bag of cookies from the store or cook up some Kool-Aid® for the potluck, she never did. It took real tact when the church ladies published a cookbook with stirring recipes of favorite potluck dishes. Delphine would have her feelings hurt if not included, so she was asked to contribute her recipe for celery sticks and peanut butter. She was so proud when the cookbook was published she gave the book to everyone as gifts with her recipe highlighted.

We all got our just deserts for our critical remarks regarding Delphine's cooking when one Sunday, following a Saturday night potluck supper, the church pews were sparsely populated. The choir had been thinned so badly they couldn't carry a tune. Even the preacher spent the day on the throne in his reading room. Despite the fact there was no conclusive evidence which dish had contained the particularly noxious strain of food poisoning, that did not stop the vicious rumors:

"I'm sure it was the mayonnaise in Letha's potato salad."

"Vera's beans were boiling and they weren't even over a flame."

To this day most survivors blame Delphine's celery sticks for forcing the pastor to cancel all future potlucks. Unofficially, he said that as long as Delphine was involved, selecting your potluck meal would always be like like playing Russian Roulette with food.

Do You Take This Horse?

A BRITISH NEWSPAPER reported that a woman replaced her girl friend as bridesmaid in her wedding with a horse. It's really not so stupid when you think about it, the bride didn't have to buy an expensive dress for her friend or worry about the bridesmaid stealing her husband. But I think the bride made the wrong substitution. She should have replaced the groom with a horse.

There's an old saying that you should never marry your horse. I think it means you should never become too attached to any creature with four legs. But I believe it would be a much better idea for a woman to marry a horse than a man. Here are just a few reasons why:

Horses don't watch Monday Night Football.

A horse husband would never leave the toilet lid up.

They may grunt when you put on a few pounds but they'll never say anything.

A horse would provide more reliable transportation than a man and you don't have to get smelly putting gas in their tank, usually.

A horse husband won't send flowers on your anniversary either.

Unlike a man, you can lead a horse to water and it will occasionally take a bath.

Horses don't belch, are more polite in public, they can go anywhere a man can and the places they go are far more interesting.

A horse will eat anything and their food can be served cold.

Horses are more obedient. A horse knows what "Whoa big fella" means.

They are bigger, stronger and look better in leather.

Most were born in a barn so they don't notice dusty furniture, dirty dishes or lint balls under the bed.

Horses don't have last names so you wouldn't have to go through life saddled with a stupid name that you hate every time you sign something.

The shoes of a horse don't cost $275 and their socks match more often than men's.

Unlike your husband, if your horse is stolen the police will actually look for it.

When a horse is said to be "broke" it does not refer to the financial condition of most potential human husbands.

Horses are not whisperers, unlike a man, they can keep a secret.

Horses don't go bald, are usually better groomed and have far better morals.

Unlike a man, they smell better when sweaty.

A horse doesn't come with a mother-in-law or a father-in-law.

Horses are more sensitive to the needs of women and don't channel surf with the remote control.

A horse husband would be just as handy around the house as a man.

They don't gamble all your hard earned money away on horse races.

Just think, if you marry a horse you can shop for silver jewelry together.

Horses improve with age and have a shorter life span, meaning you can own several in one lifetime.

Horses seldom get jealous, are better listeners, don't talk about themselves incessantly and are not descended from apes.

You can corral or tie a horse up and they are always ready when you are.

You can pet and hug a horse without it always leading to other things.

You can possess more than one legally.

Unlike your husband, if you don't like your horse you can sell it for hard cash.

BIRTHDAY PARTY

EVERY YEAR my in-laws make it a point to invite some-one to Christmas dinner who is poor, downtrodden and an outcast from society. Usually it's me, so it is no surprise when I receive a polite request every year to drive five hours one way to attend their annual Christmas feast. And I assume they are not surprised every year when I decline, always with the same excuse: "I have to stay home and feed the animals."

They invariably respond: "What a shame you have to spend Christmas with your animals."

More than 2,000 years ago another man spent what would become Christmas Day with the animals. In fact, he was born amongst them. He was not dressed in a cute little blue sailor suit or put on exhibit for everyone to see. Instead, he was wrapped in swaddling clothes and laid in a simple manger, a trough where livestock had fed. Mary and Joseph did not stay at a fancy motel with room service and halls decked with holly, but in a stable surrounded by God's creatures.

Who did the angels choose to break the news that the Savior was born that day? Lo and behold, the angels selected simple shep-herds to tell everybody what the Lord had made known to them. They had been in the field watching their flocks by night on that very first Christmas Eve.

So, I don't think it's such a bad thing that I'll spend Christmas with my best friends... the animals. If it was good enough for Jesus it's good enough for me.

I always get a joyous feeling on Christmas Day on my way to the ranch. The stores are closed and the streets are empty as I pass houses where fathers are watching football, or trying to read instructions in Taiwanese in order to put together Junior's latest toy. Grandpas are taking naps and Grandmas are, no doubt, trying to save every last scrap of wrapping paper and ribbon. Moms are doing dishes and the kids are looking for batteries. Me? I'm on my way to feed the cows, a Christmas ritual I enjoy.

Christmas is indeed a magical time of year. This Christmas I will probably give my dog a new flea collar and a few extra rubs on the belly. My horse will get a carrot and a few extra minutes of my time. I will feel a kinship with those shepherds as I check the pregnant ewes. In a few more weeks they'll be lambing and the thought of spinning tails, fuzzy fleece and legs that are too tall will cause me to smile. It always does.

I will throw out a few extra flakes of hay for the cows and their new fall-born calves who will seem cuter to me this day. I won't be in such a hurry to finish feeding. My Christmas tree won't be perfectly shaped, but it won't be plastic either. And it will be alive tomorrow, providing protection for an assortment of livestock.

I wonder if Jesus came again on this Christmas Day if he would have to stay with the animals again because the hotels would be full of tourists? Probably so. I can't imagine he'd have reservations. My in-laws would most likely invite Mary and Joseph for Christmas Dinner, them being downtrodden and all. I also wonder if the lowly shepherds were once again chosen to announce the arrival of Jesus if the media stars, who pass for reporters, would take them seriously. They probably wouldn't even bother to interrupt the football game and make a special announcement of his return. Oh well, the kids would probably rather see Santa anyway. And our modern day wise men would likely scoff at the thought that the Lord would communicate with lowly shepherds when he could have used the Internet.

But the shepherds, the cowboys and I, well, we can relate to the man and his message born more than 2,000 years ago. We see God's handiwork every day of the year... "Bright and beautiful, great and small, wise and wonderful, the Lord God made them all."

Happy Birthday, Jesus.

WHAT AM I?

THERE OUGHT TO BE a law regarding restroom signs. They should be clearly marked either "Men" or "Women" and anyone breaking this law should be forced to wait in a long line after consuming vast quantities of a liquid substance. Restaurateurs who think they are being cute by naming their rest rooms "Boars" and "Sows" or "Crowers" and "Setters" are causing a great deal of confusion, not to mention discomfort.

I think this terrible attempt at being cute started with ethnic restaurants who designated their restrooms in foreign languages like Chinese and Swahili. I'm deathly afraid to drink the water in any restaurant these days, not because the water might have life forms of an unknown origin in it, but because I might drink too much and have to use the facilities. If I guess the wrong door I might walk in on a bunch of screaming women and end up in jail or on the front page of the local newspaper as some kind of weirdo. I don't think you should have to learn a second language to use the bathroom in this country.

The growth of steak houses has really caused a lot of flushed faces. In keeping with the western theme I have seen bathrooms named Bulls, Heifers, Steers and Cows. The problem is the general public doesn't know the sex of a "Wrangler" or that "Bull Riders" are usually male and "Barrel Racers" female. If you only have a 50/50 chance of guessing right you'll just wait till you get home.

The very word "cowboy" is confusing. A "cow" is female and a "boy" is male. So what's a "cowboy" to use, "The Bull Pen" or "The Hen House?" And with women wearing pants and men wearing earrings these days you can't tell by the silhouette diagram on the door any more.

If we allow this trend to continue restaurant goers in the future are just going to have to become better educated about farm animals. Either that or face potentially embarrassing situations involving members of the opposite sex. The problem is that most people don't know the sex of a steer or whether a filly is male or female. And what is a wether anyway? See what I mean? There you are shaking in your shorts, afraid to open the door of the reading room because you don't know if you are a "Drake" or a "Duck." And we haven't even mentioned goats and shoats. I am an animal science graduate and I live in fear that some day I'll be in need of relief and have to figure out the whole donkey/mule thing. Can you imagine how difficult this all must be for an urbane liberal arts graduate under extreme duress?

It really gets confusing when they start using sheep names. When it says "Ewe" on the door don't you naturally assume it's for you? Things have gotten so confusing in San Francisco regarding the sexes that I'm told they have solved the problem with "Unisex" restrooms. As I understand it, this is some kind of hybrid or crossbred where both sexes use the same facilities. With this in mind I'd recommend that the next time you GO to Frisco that you really do... GO... before you get there.

We really do need to revert back to just plain "Men" and "Women." But even this can cause problems. I was in Sparks, Nevada, when a bunch of busy-bodies with nothing better to do than snoop around schools checking out restrooms, discovered that the bathrooms at Reed High School said "Men" and "Girls" instead of "Men" and "Women." The local women's libbers pointed out that this was sexist, and I suppose it was. But isn't that the point?

This matter desperately needs someone's immediate attention. I plead with sanitation engineers to keep it simple. Believe me, there is nothing more exasperating than standing in a crowded bar unable to use the facilities because you have just realized that you are neither a "stud" nor a "chick."

THE WONDER OF READING

WE ARE GRADUALLY saying good-bye to a generation of people who had their lives and educations interrupted by work, wars and responsibilities impossible for the rest of us to comprehend. These people are living reminders that illiteracy is not always a sign of stupidity. Oh, I know, look up the word illiterate in the dictionary and it will say things like ignorant and empty-headed. But it's not always the people who cannot read who are ignorant, but the ones who can read and don't surely are.

It's hard to imagine that some people in this technically advanced world of ours can't read the sports page, Steinbeck or Bombeck. How sad they've never curled up in the company of a good book. To write you must read and these folks will never know the satisfaction of scribbling their random thoughts, nor can they tap the wisdom of the ages recorded in books.

The unlettered have to make up for their shortcoming in other ways. They can't read the handwriting on the wall or the directions on the package so they figure things out for themselves. Like the inventor who couldn't fill out the patent applications on his many complicated inventions. Or the housewife with the unfailing memory who couldn't write a note to herself so she had to memorize the shopping list.

There is another trait the illiterate seem to share: They go to great lengths to hide their impairment. Like the dairyman who always wore a wrist watch and carried a ball point pen in his shirt pocket, even though they were as worthless to him as yesterday's newspaper. Which he couldn't read either. When asked what time it was, he'd point to his watch and say, "See for yourself." When queried as to how many cows he was milking he'd answer, "Too many to count." Which for him was true.

The untutored are reluctant to put their weakness on display for all to see. They will stare at a newspaper if only to look at the pictures or struggle over a contract as if they can read the fine print. They'll scribble their "signature" like a Doctor writing a prescription. We accept the Doctor's excuse: 21 years scrawling notes in school, but to the illiterate we extend no such understanding.

Some of the unlettered make jokes about the many advantages of illiteracy to hide their humiliation. Like the successful businessman who was not a man of letters but of numbers. He could add figures in his head nearly as fast as a calculator and could read people like a book. Too bad he couldn't write one. He rationalized, "I don't need to read what a bunch of over-educated fortune tellers have to say. They've all read so much they've gotten stupid." That may be true, but we are all diminished when books are left unread and stories untold.

I don't believe them when they claim their lives are less complicated. Certainly that's not the case of the fisherman who liked to tie flies but refused to go to the optometrist when his eyesight got fuzzy. He didn't want to admit he didn't know the letters on the eye chart so he bought his "reading glasses" off the shelf and struggled with his flies. Maybe he never wasted time reading trashy novels or took pen in hand to write bad poetry but he also missed one of the greatest joys in life: reading.

I met a man not too long ago who inspired this little essay. He was one of those who went to work at an early age and then off to the Army to fight for his country. At an advanced age he is now learning to read. "Why now?" I wondered aloud.

The old man replied, "I saw a blind man reading a book in braille and I could see on his face the great pleasure it brought him. I realized that blind man had seen much more of the world than I had."

Now every time I open a good book, read the newspaper or write a letter to a friend I am reminded to thank Dick, Jane, Spot and the teacher who taught me to read.

TOWN AND COUNTRY DOGS

IF I WERE an ice cream flavor I'd want to be vanilla. If I was reincarnated as a motor vehicle I'd be a pickup truck and if I were an animal I'd choose to be a ranch dog. I wouldn't want to be anyone's town dog because lap dogs are wimps. They usually weigh under ten pounds whereas any ranch dog that weighs under forty pounds is considered part of the cat family. The ranch dog chases cars while the city dog rides in them. The town dog has its own room but has to be let out of the house periodically for personal reasons. The country mutt's hut is under the front porch and it goes whenever and wherever it wants to.

A ranch dog will chase anything as long as somebody is willing to throw it. A town dog has the attitude of, "You threw it and now you can go get it."

A ranch dog will come when called, whereas a city dog will have you leave a message and it will get back to you at a more convenient time.

Dogs raised in the city are named Muffie, Sweetums or Princess. They wear designer outfits, have styled hair and clipped nails. They bathe on a regular basis. Country dogs are called Down Boy and Sick Em. They only get wet when an enraged city person turns the hose on them for trying to breed their poor defenseless poodle.

Town dogs are purebreds, both parents are of the same breed and have a first, middle and last name. Most ranch dogs, on the other hand, just showed up at the back porch one day. They have more scandal than spaniel in their backgrounds. To city dogs proper breeding is very important but most ranch dogs think it's fun too.

Ranch dogs chase squirrels that city dogs run from.

No country dog has ever been on an airplane.

A city dog won't do anything to help around the house, whereas ranch dogs will help wash the dishes by licking them clean. A city dog has to have its bed turned down at night. You can pet a ranch dog but make a move towards a city dog and it will bite your ankle.

When city dogs get sick their owners take them to a small animal specialist. If a ranch dog gets sick his only chance of being seen by a veterinarian is if the vet glances in the dog's direction when he comes to preg check the cows. Ranch dogs get distemper whereas city dogs get "canine influenza." Farm dogs have an average life expectancy of 15 years and the usual cause of death is from following a car or cow too closely. City dogs die from hardening of the arteries at the grand old age of 7. They are buried in pet cemeteries.

Ranch dogs eat once a day if they are lucky. If anybody actually gives them food their first reaction is to bury it. City dogs eat formulated and complex diets and actually get to eat the food that is brought home in doggie bags.

Admittedly, city dogs have more social graces than ranch dogs. They don't slobber or lick themselves in public places. To them a parking meter is a place to be tied while the mistress is shopping. To a ranch dog a parking meter is a pay toilet. Ranch dogs have been known to jump on you after running through a cow pasture.

But I still like them better.

Ranch dogs make much better watch dogs. A city dog needs a burglar alarm to alert it if someone is stealing the family silver. Their first reaction is to hide or play dead. A ranch dog's reaction is much more aggressive. Depending on the breed they will either gather them up or "point." A city dog is much too polite to point. This is a shame because if you live in a big city you need a good watch dog to protect you from people you never would meet if you lived in the country!

PARENTS ONCE REMOVED

I MISS MY grandparents. I think my whole baby-boom generation does. For some reason I've always preferred the company of my grandparent's generation. Old people. Now that I'm becoming one I'm beginning to understand why. Looking back now it's obvious they always provided the most sage advice, the best example and the purest love.

I'd like to say a few nice words about Grandmas and Grandpas. And I'd better hurry because they're dying off, you know? I'm buying sympathy cards by the box and my funeral suit is looking threadbare. Sadly, many of the Grandmas and Grandpas still with us are hiding in Alzheimer's world: disremembering and refusing to accept the present. And who can blame them with what we've done with the place. They gave us a more educated, leisurely and peaceful world and we turned it into a bad soap opera. We're all too busy playing Who Wants To Be A Millionaire to straighten up the joint.

Oh, I know, new Grandparents are being made every day. But not like the ones you and I had. Those wonderful fuddy-duddies who managed somehow to live without colored underwear, call waiting, blue M & M's and the World Wide Web. They're going to be hard to replace.

There was a time in my life when it was easy to dismiss the blue haired old ladies and liver spotted curmudgeons as relics from the past. "Hey, you there in the big boat of a car, get off the road. Time has passed you by." We laugh at them for continuing to make their own ice cubes when the refrigerator will do it for them. We ridicule their old fashioned values. You don't really need a husband to have a baby any more and kids can be raised at Child Care Incorporated. But gradually we are starting to realize the joke may be on us. Turns out they knew something we didn't. How could that possibly be?

To be fair, I suppose it's hard to know your real grandparents if you never met your father or you were conceived in a petri dish from an unknown donor. So, for those unfortunate souls who never got to know theirs, I'd like to describe what a grandparent is.

They are parents once removed. Like parents, only more so.

In many ways Grandparents are more understanding. Sure, they may not like the earring in your ear but they'll still stop in the grocery store to show off your school picture to a total stranger. They may not particularly like the fact that your new boyfriend or girlfriend has purple hair, or you are dating at sixteen, but they also remember that they were already married by then. They know you'll make mistakes in life because they did. They turned out all right and you will too.

Above all a good grandparent is a good listener. Admittedly, half the time you don't know if they can hear you because their hear-ing-aid is turned off, or, if they've drifted off to sleep, having heard it all before. But at least they take the time to listen. Somehow they know your load will be lighter having shared it.

Grandparents are as predictable as teenage acne. Every birthday you can expect a card with money in it. Not much though. Grandparents don't understand the ravages inflation can play on a child's allowance. Probably because they lived through the Great Depression. As I understand it, there was nothing "great" about it. So, pardon them now if you have to sneak back and leave a bigger tip for the waitress when they take you out to eat.

My grandparents were creatures of habit who lived by everyday rituals. They were happy with who they were, where they were. They weren't obsessed with climbing any ladder and material possessions did not possess them. I used to think their lives were boring, now as my own world becomes more like theirs, I find it serene. Funny, as I've gotten older my grandparents became a lot smarter. Someday I hope to be as good as them. It's a lofty goal, I know. That's why they're called Grand...parents.

ODDS AND ENDS

I KNEW SOMETHING was wrong from the beginning. It was a very difficult birth and the calf was real slow getting up. She kept falling down all rubbery legged, even more than usual. It seemed the cow was losing hope. She needed her calf to live. A cow will usually survive a difficult calving if she has a calf to care for. After the birth we didn't know if the calf had lived or died because the mother hid it for more than a week. Looking back now, I guess the cow was ashamed of her inferior calf.

We called the heifer Palsy because she shook a lot. I just figured she'd grow out of it. The hump in her back was not apparent at that point in her life but as she grew older it became obvious that Palsy was special. At weaning time we gathered the herd and there was Palsy struggling to keep up at the end of the line, walking sideways. The arch in her back was becoming more pronounced. It was my intent to load her up with the rest of the calves and ship her to the auction market. But a big pair of pleading, soulful eyes convinced me that I would not ship her... and that was just the look on my wife's face. Palsy looked even more pathetic.

"We can't go on keeping all the odds and ends," I told my wife.

"Why not? She's not hurting anything. Besides you keep a lot of other misfits around," as she pointed to Gentleman, my horse, who was sharing a flake of hay with Palsy. She was splayed out in the feed bunk. All the other animals seemed to like Palsy.

It was true. I had kept other worthless animals around. I had a three legged ram and an impotent bull. There was my cat who was afraid of mice and my watchdog Aussie. I had to admit if there was a suspicious noise I had to wake her up to bark. And of course, Gentleman, my horse. But at least they all had a purpose. It was not the same with Palsy.

A couple of weeks later my wife and I were sharing a spot of tea in our local bakery when once again the subject of Palsy came up.

"What will we do with her?" I asked my wife. "We can't keep her forever. Surely the bulls won't breed her and what if she did reproduce? We could have an epidemic on our hands."

"We could try to sell her," my wife suggested. "But whoever buys her has to promise her a good home."

"Are you kidding? Nobody is going to buy her."

"We could donate her to charity or put her up for adoption," pleaded my soft-hearted wife. "We could have a "Name the Heifer Contest." Palsy isn't a very good name really. And whoever wins the contest gets to keep her for the rest of her life."

"I'm not any happier about this than you are," I said. "We really should just send her to the auction but I really don't want anybody seeing our brand on her."

"She isn't branded," recalled my wife. "She kept falling down in the chute when you tried to brand her, remember? But anyway, I don't want everybody laughing at her when she walks sideways into the auction ring."

Just then, a crippled old man with a crooked back limped into the bakery. At the counter he turned his pocket inside out which brought forth some lint and twelve cents. "What will that buy?" he asked the clerk. The young girl behind the counter gave him a day-old donut and a smile. He shuffled out the door with his donut.

We decided that day to keep Palsy. It was my way of buying that man a cup of coffee to go with his donut.

THE SYNDROME SYNDROME

I'VE BEEN HANGING around a lot of medical doctors lately and the more I do, the more I appreciate veterinarians. In many ways the vet's job is much more difficult. Veterinarians must diagnose diseases without being able to ask the patient where it hurts and without doing all sorts of procedures, like cat scans and barium enemas. The only time a vet recommends "barium" is if the patient died.

Animal doctors don't call in specialists for every little part of the anatomy either. They wear coveralls, don't hang all their diplomas in their truck and they aren't full of themselves. And veterinarians don't get all pushed out of shape if you don't refer to them as "Doctor." They don't take Wednesdays off to play golf or leave you waiting in an office, reading old magazines until you die of natural causes. Veterinarians still make house calls and most can write legibly. The only time MD's scrawl plainly is when they write you out a bill for services rendered.

People doctors could learn a lot from animal docs. Such as how to talk. Medical doctors like to use real long words in telling you what's wrong with you, so that they can charge you about $1,000 per syllable to treat you. They use words like "myocardial infarction" and "antigen." My Aunt Jen had an infarction once and all we did was air out the house. Didn't cost a thing except for the room deodorant.

Vets call it like they see it. Maladies like wooden tongue, foot rot, overeating disease, lump jaw and pinkeye need no further explanation. When's the last time your MD diagnosed you with slobbers or the squirts? No, they have to give you a long name of a rare and expensive disorder. If they diagnosed you with something simple, like shipping fever, they could not refer you to their specialist brother-in-law.

Take horses, for instance. Veterinarians have simplified equine medicine to the point where there are only five things that can possibly go wrong with a horse. Either the patient has sleeping sickness, the shakes, worms, colic or a "hitch in its get-a-long." The way a good vet treats these problems is by a good worming or by floating the teeth. Any veterinarian will tell you there's no sense in spending a lot of extra money on a horse that's got its mind set on dying. That may sound cruel but it's better than what medical doctors put humans through. Six weeks of exhaustive tests only to be diagnosed with chronic fatigue syndrome. You'll soon discover that when a doctor doesn't know what's wrong with you he'll call it a "syndrome." If a medical doctor looked at a steer with bloat you can bet your stethoscope he'd call it Irritable Bowel Syndrome.

There's another thing that really gets under my skin about medical doctors. I've always been amazed how you can go to the same

Doctor once a month for years and they never remember what's wrong with you without looking at your chart. A veterinarian, on the other hand, is apt to remember every animal on the ranch. "Oh, that's the cow that kicked me in the shin when I was pregnancy examining her."

The best part about veterinarians is they give instructions that are easy to follow. "Rub some of this free sample stuff on that sore twice a day." Or, "Put some blue pills down its throat and forget it." If the situation is hopeless they don't beat around the bush or give you the bad news in small doses, as if they were milking a cash cow. I suppose an MD can't come right out and say, "If I were you I'd have the tallow man on standby." Or, "We ought to just put the old wind bag out of her misery." But they could be a little more honest and forthcoming once in awhile.

I think I've finally figured out why veterinarians make matters so much more simple, less expensive, with far less paper work than medical doctors.

Animals don't normally have health insurance!

DUCK HERDIN' DOG

LIKE EVERYONE ELSE, we have a few status symbols in the livestock business and a good dog is one of them.

We bought our status symbol at a Kelpie stud in Australia. I told the owner, Carl, that I wanted a good cow dog; something to match wits with a progressive cattlemen such as myself. He showed my wife and I his prize winning dog who could walk over the backs of sheep in a corral and understood the English language, at least the way Australians speak it. He then showed us a litter that had just whelped out of a champion bitch. Naturally, I bought one.

I came back to America and waited anxiously for the quarantine period to come to a close. After what seemed like an eternity, Aussie, our new dog arrived from Australia. Now, the dog that finally arrived was either not related to the dogs I had seen down under or something was lost in the translation. She couldn't herd a dim-witted calf.

I complained by phone to Carl but he replied, "Aye, bloke, she's not a cattlemen's dog. She's opened her eyes and seen the light. She's a sheep dog now!"

So, I had to buy some sheep. And some ducks. The ducks, you see, are what you use to train a good sheep dog. The idea is to get three ducks, put them in a round pen and then walk around the outside of that pen with the dog on the opposite side. The goal is to get the dog to circle the pen and keep the ducks in a straight line between you and the dog. In no time Aussie became a world champion duck herder. Soon Aussie was herding ducks everywhere, 10 hours a day. Those ducks must have felt like a henpecked husband!

Aussie was now ready for the next step: sheep. Unfortunately, I soon discovered that Aussie was afraid of the woolly creatures. This is not a good trait for a sheep dog to have! A black faced ewe stamped her foot and made threatening gestures towards Aussie and she ran away from home for two weeks. The ducks had never stamped their feet at her in such a manner.

I decided to lay off the heavy training for awhile and just teach Aussie the normal things that all good dogs should know: Like house training, begging, shaking hands, rolling over and playing dead.

One daring day I took Aussie out with me into the cow pasture. When a large, horned cow with a nasty disposition cornered Aussie in the corral it was then that Aussie really showed her training. First she begged for mercy, then she attempted to shake hands with the cow and finally decided just to roll over and play dead.

Aussie is not even proficient at riding around in the back of the truck looking like a status symbol. She keeps jumping out to chase squirrels. She also loves to roll in fresh cow manure and is the only dog

I know that actually smells better after having done so.

Aussie barks and wakes me up every morning at three and she hides under the house and whimpers during thunderstorms or when airplanes fly overhead. I can't even take her to other ranch roundups to show her off because she is so hyperactive. One rancher said me bringing my dog to a branding is "like losing three good men." Meanwhile I suffer the scoffs in silence waiting for Aussie's talents to ripen.

But one day recently I had one fleeting flash of status. The ducks got out of their pen and had to be put back in. It was Aussie's proudest moment.

FAMILY MATTERS

IF I COULD change one thing in this world it would be to give every kid a family. Not a "new math" family with five half-brothers and sisters, two part time stepmoms and a father who is missing in action. Those fractions add up to a "nuclear family" that could blow apart any global village; dividing as fast as it is multiplying. I'm thinking more of a traditional family with two parents, some brothers and sisters, a couple grandparents, a crazy old uncle and maybe a dog. I would not waste my one wish on wealth or welfare because a family like that can make a happy home out of any old hut.

If I were society's architect I'd start with parents: two of them. The father and mother roles would be played by a man and a woman because women still make the best moms and men the best dads. This would be the basis for what used to be known as the "family unit," before the monetary unit took its place. One dedicated father and one loving mother: What a concept! The idea may be out of fashion but it's still the best form of government ever devised and the source of greatest human happiness.

The parents would spend more time selecting their lifelong partner than they would their silver pattern and would be willing to finish any family they started. Their long range plans would include staying together instead of going from matrimony to alimony before the first child is born. No child of theirs would be shuttled back and forth between parents on an airplane like some piece of excess baggage. Or have their IRS deductibility argued over in court.

These old fashioned parents would spend more time investing in the family than in the NASDAQ and would talk to their kids more often than their stockbroker. They'd give their children a safety net and a head start in life by teaching them a trade, manners and sportsmanship at an early age. They'd be more concerned about being a good parent and less about being a pal. They wouldn't give their kids a new car to drive to school that is better than their teachers can afford. And if a child was overly interested in things that go boom the parents would be the first to know. Not the last.

I wonder, is it asking too much for prospective parents to realize that bringing a child into the world includes some responsibilities that should NOT be handed off to a day care center, Internet chat room, school system or penal institution?

In rebuilding the family's foundation I'd surely want to include some brothers and sisters as building blocks. Hopefully there would be at least two offspring so they could learn to share their toys, teachers, communicable diseases and inner-most thoughts. Siblings simply can't be beat as teachers for life's most important lessons: Knock first. Clean up your own mess. Pass the gravy, please. It's always your turn to do the dishes.

As they've been known to do on occasion brothers and sisters will no doubt combat, compete, compromise and tattle-tale over trivial things. And hopefully those things not so trifling; like a brother experimenting with drugs or a sister hanging with the wrong crowd. Sure, they can be annoying at times but siblings guarantee two things in life: a high phone bill and a friend forever.

No family would be complete without a full complement of supporting players: grandparents to spoil the children rotten, cousins to take the place of gang members, and plenty of aunts and uncles who enjoy sitting at the folding table with the little tykes for Sunday dinners or holidays. Is there anything better than a family that's all wrapped up with one another on Christmas Day? What's the point of having a sap in the family tree if he is known only by his name badge? Or a doting aunt who is recognized only for traveling the farthest distance to the reunion?

Want to live in a better world? Then remember this: Family matters.

HIS AND HERS

HAVE YOU NOTICED that more and more women are driving pickup trucks these days? But have you also noticed there is a big difference in the trucks that men and women drive? Here are some variations I've noticed.

In many ways women are just like their wheels: chromed with excellent tread. Men's tires reflect their personality too: balding and so wide they have to be purchased from a farm implement dealer.

In a man's mind a pickup truck is not a truck unless you have to strain yourself to climb in or use a rope ladder. A woman wants running boards.

Women like shiny new paint and pin stripes. Men consider primer a final coat.

A man wants four on the floor whereas a woman has to have automatic transmission, power brakes and independent rear suspension.

Optional equipment on a woman's truck includes a lighted makeup mirror and curtains. Optional equipment in a man's truck includes a spit cup, fog lights, roll bar and mud flaps.

In a man's truck the term "dual exhaust" has a double meaning.

Either he has two tail pipes or another male passenger.

A woman has to have the interior covered with a pastel shade of shag carpeting. A man's interior is wall to wall rubber so that the inside can be cleaned out with a high pressure hose.

A woman has never actually slept in the "bed" of her truck.

The term "under the hood" means different things to men and women. To a man it means an enjoyable day playing in grease. To a woman it means spending a day at the beauty shop.

Open the glove compartment in a man's truck and you'll find a pre-pop top bottle opener, a roll of toilet paper, an assortment of old speeding tickets and the skeleton of a dead fish from the last time he was allowed to go fishing and forgot what he did with his catch. Open the glove compartment of his wife's truck and you will find at least three tubes of lipstick, the current truck registration, insurance forms and an assortment of maps for the county, state and nation. (Men don't need maps because they never get lost, can't refold them and their wives are always around to tell them where to go.)

On the back of a woman's truck you'll find bumper stickers that refer to cosmetics, saving whales and the fact that their child is an honor student. On the back of a real man's truck are bumper snickers that read: Nuke the Whales, He Who Dies with the Most Toys Wins, and My Kid Can Beat Up Your Honor Student.

A woman never goes a week without washing her truck. The

last time a man's truck got rinsed was when he accidentally backed his bass boat trailer a little too far into the lake at the boat ramp.

In a man's truck the radio is preset to sports talk radio and country music stations. A woman's is set to easy listening, financial news, road conditions, traffic reports and some celebrity shrink.

Look at a man's truck and you will see a cracked windshield, a side mirror sitting on the dash, radio speakers from an old drive-in and a clothes hanger radio antennae that also serves as an extra set of keys when he locks himself out of the truck. Which is quite often. The upholstery is covered in food stains, grease and cigarette burns. The bed of the truck is full of his beer can collection and all of his other material possessions.

Look at a woman's pickup and you'll probably find fluffy woolen seat covers, an air deodorizer hanging from the rear view mirror, working windshield wipers and turn signals that occasionally seem to be hooked up backwards.

AND THEN WE WONDER, "WHY?"

WE GIVE OUR kids well-armed action fighting figures to play with and video games where they point pretend guns at play people and then we are surprised when they aim real guns at real people. We idolize toilet mouthed rappers who "sing" of shooting their mothers and then we are shocked when they do. We glorify guns and celebrate a culture of death with music, movies and TV all under the guise of "free speech." And then we are shocked speechless when life imitates what passes for "art." Kids shoot kids, they die and then we wonder, "WHY?"

We have become so politically correct everything is now okay. We put more effort into saving three legged frogs than we do tattooed teenagers. Our answer to abhorrent behavior is to pass out free needles and condoms. Our playwrights, pundits and politicians don't want to offend anyone so they indulge everyone. We have created a culture that doesn't have any. We free the whales, the wolves and the criminals. We have commercialized Santa Claus, put the Tooth Fairy on the Forbes 400 and created some monsters who would gun down the

Easter Bunny. And we wonder, "WHY?"

We assassinate the character of would be role-models and create celebrities out of rappers with records and athletes with rap sheets. We name murderers and thugs our Most Valuable Players. The only "Most Wanted" list they're on is for interviews and autographs. Drug dealers and white collar criminals are pardoned while truth tellers are assaulted and attacked. Our government says gambling is bad for everyone except state governments. The only goals and dreams we've given our children are just to leave school in something other than a body bag. And we wonder, "WHY?"

We are titillated by shock jocks, the "reality" of TV shows and nightly soap operas where everyone is single, neurotic and lives in a New York City apartment. The networks try to soar to the top of the ratings by reaching low into the gutter. They don't glorify goodness because it doesn't move the merchandise. Our best selling books are written by people who never read any. We celebrate depravity daily. Spies and lies lead the evening news and we wonder, "WHY?"

Our schools have turned into shooting galleries for both drugs and guns. When kids misbehave these days a single parent threatens to count to ten, but they never get beyond three. If the bad behavior continues the kids are put on drugs to calm them down, and then we wonder why they become addicts later in life. We think stupidity and sloth are caused by a lack of government funding. We blame the teachers or send the kids to the mall because it's easier than helping with homework. We turn the raising of our children over to the global village because no one else is home. We tie up the dog but let the kids run wild. Families talk in chat rooms but not family rooms. We kicked prayer out of schools, muddied the line between right and wrong and only hope that God grades on a curve. Jesus can't get past the metal detectors. And we wonder, "Why is this happening?"

We pay our shortstops and jump shooters millions while our teachers get peanuts. We've sold our kids to Wall Street marketing wizards who "target" their demographic like a grade school sniper. Talk show evangelists tell us we really can have everything. We have taught our kids that money comes from ATM machines, not hard work. We lecture them about the dangers of drugs, alcohol and pot while we blow smoke in their face. They can smell the hypocrisy on our breath. We are guided not by what is proper but by what Johnny's mother lets him get away with. We try to buy our children's love with cash, cars and credit cards and they respond with anger and hostility.

And then we wonder, "WHY?"

A Newcomer's Guide To The Country

IT SEEMS LIKE more and more people are moving to the country and immediately trying to transform it into the big city they couldn't wait to escape. I should warn these modern day pioneers, there are big differences between "here" and "there." Here are a few tips to make the move easier for the invading hordes.

Don't ever try to pet the nice doggy in the back of the pickup truck, don't feed the deer or complain about any rain that might fall from the sky. Do not write letters to the editor of the weekly newspaper saying what a "hick town" your new home is. While it may be all right for us to call it that, a newcomer never should. (A newcomer is considered anyone who was not born here.) In these parts the words, "It's good cow country," are considered highly complimentary.

If a 4-H'er outside the Post Office asks if you want to buy a raffle ticket you'd better do so. Word travels fast in these parts and there are no secrets. Within two weeks we'll all know what kind of liquor you drink and how much you smoke from the clerk at the store. This information is not considered rumor or gossip.

There is an entirely different pecking order in the country where mountain lion trappers are more highly valued than lawyers. And there's a greater need for them too. Don't make jokes about bankers either, because the local one is probably a respected member of the community. If someone does something nice for you, like pull you out of a ditch or bring your lost dog back home, DO NOT offer them money. It's an insult. Baking them a nice pie, however, is acceptable. But only if you can cook.

A few words about driving in our neck of the woods: If the driver of an oncoming vehicle waves two fingers at you above the steering wheel he's not flashing you the peace symbol. The driver is just being friendly. Granted, this may be an entirely new experience for you, but learn to expect it. For example, when you stop at a four way stop and another driver waves you through even though you technically were not there first, it is perfectly all right to accept this kindness. Although you should acknowledge the courtesy in some manner, like flashing the peace sign. You'll also make the appalling discovery that out here in the hinterlands people actually observe red lights and road warnings most of the time. That's because the caution signs may indicate an oncoming coal train or a huge combine on the road ahead.

Leave your consumptive snobbery back in the city. We don't care about the year and model of the car you drive. Besides, our dirty, dusty roads play heck with black foreign cars, ladies lathered in greasy makeup and guys who plaster their hair with gel or mousse. The only moose out here are the ones that may run out in front of your car at night when you are least expecting it.

When dining out don't ask for anything on the half-shell or order an argula salad with brie dressing. We'll all be embarrassed for you if you eat your chicken with a knife and fork, or your chicken fried steak with your fingers. We do not consider asking for a wine steward a sign of sophistication, especially if you're at the Dairy Queen. We don't have a sushi bar but the grocery store does sell bait, along with calf replacer, horseshoe nails and mineral blocks.

We speak a different dialect too. In our world the FFA has nothing to do with Federal Aviation or the NRA with nurses. And there are a few things you should NEVER say or we'll know you're not a native species. Don't ask for the recipe for a cow pie or where you can buy a sweater for your Dachshund. Never ask, "What's that smell?" Or, "Do you have a local Sierra Club Chapter?" Never, ever, refer to coyotes as "cute."

If you want to survive your move to the country NEVER say no to a potluck or yes if a neighbor offers zucchini from their garden. Other than that, you're on your own. Good luck... you are going to need it.

MISFITS

LET'S TRY A LITTLE experiment. Please think back and try to recall the most unforgettable characters that you have ever raised. I am not talking about your children here, although I'm sure there are times you'd like to forget that they are yours. No, I am talking about the animals that you have pictures of in your scrapbook and fond memories of in your hearts. Are you thinking of them?

I bet they were misfits.

I don't mean the three-headed or six legged kind of misfits, but animals that just didn't seem to fit, that stood apart from the herd.

The stories I've written that readers tell me they like the best are the ones about such misfits. Of course there is my horse Gentleman, but you also seemed to find a place in your hearts for my alcoholic pig, the babysitting cow and Two Car, that pathetic calf that had to spend his first two weeks of its life in my garage.

They were all round pegs in square holes. They were the ones with personality and when you think of them a smile creeps across your face and when they died your whole day was ruined. They were the bummer lambs that spent two days on your hearth and six weeks in your way. They were the foals that walked sideways or the calves that tried to run on two legs. If they were children they'd be wearing padded helmets and be confined to a wheelchair.

We all still have them even though farm economists have told us they are not efficient. Even today the animal in my menagerie that comes to mind first is a misfit.

Stubby is a real body of work, literally a dead end. I don't really know how my bull lost his tail, he just came that way. When I see Stubby standing by himself I can just hear the other cattle laughing at him, and I must admit that I have too on occasion. After all, when my tailless bull raises his stump he looks like a very large German Shorthair attempting to flush a covey of quail. But during fly season I don't laugh at him, I feel sorry for him. The flies realize that Stubby can't do anything about it, so for five months every year they use his back as an aircraft carrier. It is a pitiful sight indeed watching him swish his stub in vain.

I have tried to put fly tags in his ears but he only has stubs for ears. They must have froze off the same time his tail did. I tried to rig up a prosthetic tail made from a piece of rope and a mop but he got it caught in the fence and left it hanging from the top wire.

As if not possessing all the necessary appendages was bad enough, the parts Stubby does have are all messed up. Someone must have put his horn weights on wrong when he was a calf because today one horns points straight south and the other points north. Other than that Stubby is a great looking bull, he stays home and he's gentle as a lamb. Misfits usually are.

Upon seeing Stubby in our front pasture one day as the supplement salesman drove up the driveway, he asked my wife why she would keep such an ugly beast around. Just then I walked up, the salesman took one look at me and seemed to understand. But my wife answered him anyway.

"Because misfits are special," she said as she put her arm in mine.

AN OLD FAMILY RECIPE

I'D LIKE TO SHARE with you an old family recipe handed down to me that friends and relatives have enjoyed for several generations. This all time favorite is usually served on holidays or Sunday dinner but it goes well any day of the week.

Here's a list of the primary ingredients: an overflowing cup of wife, a tiny teaspoon of husband, a full measure of kids to lick the icing bowl or ice cream dashers, carefully sifted members of your extended family and a pinch of assorted friends. Preparation time is measured by the four quarters of a football game occupying the men folk in the next room. At all times during the mixing of this meal be careful not to stir them up or shake them or they might boil over into the kitchen.

Blend all these ingredients together in a home wrapped in love and basted with humor. (No maids, caterers or frozen pies please.) To decide how many you want to serve consider your budget, time and patience and then go ahead and invite everyone. Figure on three servings per person and then double the recipe.

The main dish is the host who brings everything together with five people looking over her shoulder at all times, several kids underfoot demanding to know when dinner will be ready, a dog looking for a handout and at least two men gnawing on bones over the sink. Please be advised it's the only time they'll get near the sink all day. (But you already knew that.)

The woman of the house is responsible for slapping the hand of the man of the house with a wooden spoon when he sticks his fingers in places they shouldn't be. Like a bowl full of mashed potatoes or icing on a cake. The chef should be careful not to pound too vigorously on him but he should be whisked out of the kitchen at high speed. For even better results the man should be marinated in wine prior to the meal to take the bitter edge off. Try to be short at least one key ingredient, preferably whipped cream, so that the woman can toss the man out of the house by sending him to the store. Hopefully more than once. In this way he'll feel kneaded. Other than pouring the wine, making sure the chip bowl is full and the occasional remedial carving chore, this pretty much summarizes the role of the husband of the house.

The trickiest ingredient in this old family recipe is the mother-in-law who tends to keep things shook up by grating on the cook with a vinegary tirade for three hours at 365 degrees. She should be given just enough of a job to keep her occupied, like peeling onions, while at the same time not being given enough responsibility so she can claim any responsibility whatsoever for the quality of the meal.

Saucy conversation should be stirred into the mix with the

addition of assorted sisters, neighbors and friends who just happen to drop by because they were in the neighborhood and knew something was cooking. For best results they should be added slowly to the concoctions.

Season to taste with equal parts of an assortment of relatives. Garnish with sage wisdom from Grandma, a measure of thyme from Grandpa and a little spice from an uncle who always acts like a ham at family gatherings. To keep things hot and ready-to-serve be careful to keep all dishes covered to prevent them from being disturbed by pesky aunts wearing aprons.

If you follow these step-by-step instructions you'll find that everything tastes better when served in a good home surrounded by family and friends. With a dinner thus prepared, a good cook can put up with anything, even relatives. When the last piece of pie is finished and the men are all stuffed and sleeping off their meal what you'll be left with is a messy kitchen, a recipe for happiness and leftover feelings of love and friendship that will be remembered long after the dirty dishes are finally done.

DOGGONE

WHERE, OH WHERE had my little dog gone? I had raised her from a pup and she had been a loyal companion for twelve years. That was before she decided she needed a vacation and wanted to see the world in her declining years. Maybe it was a mid-life crises or maybe it was the thunder and lightning that made her want to jump out the window.

The only other time that Aussie had been lost was when I unknowingly locked her in the shop for two days. But this was different. We searched all over the ranch but deep in my heart I knew she had headed where the trees are far apart. Aussie had taken her love to town.

Aussie had led a sheltered life. The only dogs she had ever met were other cow dogs. I would guess she didn't know there was any other kind. I was worried sick at the thought of her running with hound dogs, bull dogs and poodles, perish the thought.

In search of our dog my wife and I prowled the neighborhoods in town trying to think like a dog. When we were home we thought we should be out looking and when we were out looking we wondered if we shouldn't be home by the phone. We put ads in the paper and signs on posts but to no avail. Aussie never had learned to read. As each day passed we felt more hopeless. I began looking alongside the shoulder of the road.

Then we began frequenting the county dog pound. It seems that the terrible thunder storms had filled the place up. We met all kinds of interesting dogs there. English Sheepdogs, a Russian Afghan, a Great Dane and an Irish Wolfhound held court over the Dog United Nations. Even a Bloodhound had gotten lost and they are the dogs people send out to find lost souls. There was a retriever looking to be retrieved and a hitchhiking pointer who got picked up. There were toy dogs, beagles and bird dogs all looking to be transferred to a new post. There were police dogs in plain clothes and wiener dogs, half a dog high by a dog and a half long. But the saddest dogs of all were the little puppies that had been abandoned. They had three days to live unless adopted. By the way, the dogs with licenses had a much better chance.

When we had almost given up hope the pound people called us. Aussie shared a pen with an unlicensed dog that was glad to have company. Aussie wore a tag around her neck that was like those old brass numbers worn by dairy cows. She was number 189. We bailed her out and took her home. She was exhausted and we were elated.

After Aussie's town odyssey she was a more worldly dog and much more cosmopolitan. However, our new renaissance dog had picked up some bad habits from the town dogs. The sporting dogs taught her to chase cats and cars, and the poodles taught her to be snooty. The setters taught her to set. It was obvious she had not met any working dogs.

I wish dogs could talk so I could find out where Aussie had been and what she had done on her sabbatical. There are occasional clues. Somebody told us they saw her at the high school playing with some kids. And once in awhile she will notice something out the truck window and get a far away look in her eye like maybe she remembers a place or a time. I don't know if Aussie preferred the town life or if her great escape had taught her there is no place like home.

Meanwhile, I keep thinking about those puppies in the pound.

SOME OF MY BEST FRIENDS SMELL

I MUST ADMIT that some of my best friends are not politically correct or always in fashion. Some wear wool in July while others wear leather from head to foot. How they have escaped being picketed by animal rightists I haven't a clue.

On the other hand, many of my comrades were the first to buy into fashionable trends such as natural child birth, nude sun bathing, doing a little grass and cleansing with mud. This is hard for me to admit, but most of my best friends are vegetarians! They often dine on alfalfa sprouts, organically grown grains, expensive water in outdoor settings while barefoot with flowers in their hair.

Those of you who know me won't find it hard to believe that many of my friends lack refinement and social graces. My best buddies never say excuse me, thank you or please. They burp at will, chew with their mouths open and often drink milk straight from the spout. They scratch when and wherever it itches. Some of my best friends smell so bad they attract flies, but if I were to bring it to their attention they'd just growl and scowl, suggesting I mind my own business.

The hygiene habits of many of my friends leave a little to be desired. They seldom bathe and could accurately be described as "deodorantly deprived." Caring little about their appearance, some of my cohorts are missing half their teeth and have more hair growing in their ears than on the top of their heads. My wife finds many of my pals so disgusting that she says we all were born in a barn.

I must admit that several of my best buddies are not perfect citizens. There is not a Rhodes Scholar in the bunch, they never vote and their pedigrees hardly qualify them as blue bloods. They'd be kicked out of any country club in the country. They try their best not to work, seldom hold down steady jobs and can often be found begging for handouts, appearing dirty, unkempt and often. They spend most of their time laying around like a football fan during the playoffs, getting up only for snacks. If you laid all my overweight friends end to end, well, I'm sure they'd all be a lot more comfortable.

Family values? Forget it. I have several deadbeat dads as friends who routinely cheat on their current love interests. Most of my male cronies are more than willing to let the females do all of the work. I have some real studs as friends who stay out all hours of the night chasing females, racing fast cars and sowing more than their fair share of wild oats.

When I think about it I don't know why I keep my friends. They never call me on the telephone and I can count on one hand the times they have remembered my birthday. But on the other hand, not one of these friends has ever sent me a Christmas card letter bragging about their family, which is one of the reasons I like my friends so much. That and the fact they can ride shotgun in the truck for hours without once telling me how to drive. My friends are totally honest, never lie to me, at no time do they talk about me behind my back, and they have never turned me into the IRS. At least that I am aware of. Most of my acquaintances don't smoke, drink, gamble or borrow. They aren't just fair weather friends either and I always know where to find them when I need them.

Some of my best buddies have four legs while others have only three. Any farmer or rancher knows that missing appendages are the price one has to pay for hanging around tractors, horses and squeeze chutes. Admittedly, some of my best friends are a pain in the behind and alternately can be piggish, sheepish and bull headed.

Yes, some of my best friends are real animals.

SITTIN' WITH THE KIDS

FOR MANY A YOUNG boy the onset of puberty is celebrated with the first shave, even if there isn't a blade in the razor. I'm told that when girls come of age their interests change from softball, climbing trees and dolls, to boys, frilly dresses and makeup. But for me I knew that I had become a man the first time I didn't have to sit at the kid's table for Thanksgiving dinner. It was one of the happiest days of my life; that day I was invited to join the grown-ups for the Thanksgiving meal.

Oddly, sitting with the old people proved to be a big letdown. I found their conversation boring and their insistence on good table manners a bit too confining. I have never quite enjoyed Thanksgiving as much as when I was extradited to the kid's table by my mother.

When the relatives showed up at our house for Turkey Day all the young kids were shuttled off to the kitchen to eat. Our parents always told us it was because there wasn't enough room around the dining room table, but I also remember my mother thanking God for at least one peaceful meal a year.

To be segregated in such a manner was demoralizing for us youngsters and to further humiliate us a large plastic sheet was placed under the table just in case we might spill something. Although, as I recall, most of the food and drink was dropped in the other room.

These days when it's time for my wife and I to decide where we will freeload for Thanksgiving dinner my decision is always based on the seating arrangements. We always go where I can sit at the kid's table. They are preferred company. I don't have to worry about etiquette or the proper fork to use and no one seems to mind if I talk with my mouth open. And the conversation is much more stimulating than listening to Aunt Sis talk about her bunions or Chet his earthworms.

The best part about sitting with the kids is that you don't have to eat yams, cranberry sauce or giblet gravy if you don't want to. And the bubbly apple cider that we pretend is champagne has a much better flavor than the finest wine when shared with nieces and nephews. A Thanksgiving dinner with the kids is much more enjoyable because you can sit wherever you like. You don't have to worry about sitting in assigned seats so that certain warring factions of the family don't sit next to one another and get into yet another hostile debate on the merits of white meat versus dark.

Invariably it happens... halfway through dinner it dawns on the old folks that the main thing they have to be thankful for is having far too much fun in the next room. By the time dessert rolls around the parents in the dining room will have had about all the peace and quiet they can stand for one year. They will go to the kitchen to check on their young ones and return with them in tow. The grown-ups will make some flimsy excuse for returning with their child such as, "They were throwing mash potatoes at each other," or, "They were stuffing peas up their noses."

But the real reason the kids were brought into the dining room is because the grown-ups forgot to say grace and none of the older folks can remember a suitable prayer. Giving thanks at Thanksgiving is kid's work it seems, even if it is after the fact. So, one by one everyone will join hands, and then one very special, embarrassed, cute little kid will say grace, confusing the Pledge of Allegiance, a drinking toast learned from a deranged Uncle and a prayer taught in Sunday School.

"Dear God, hollered be thy name. Bless this house oh Lord we pray, make it safe by night and day. Thank you for the birds that sing, thank you God for everything. And thank you God for mommy and daddy and please don't tell them that we ate leftover Halloween candy for dinner and fed the turkey meat to the dog. Amen."

GOPHER FUNERALS

SOME OF MY EARLIEST memories are of gopher funerals presided over by my Uncle Mac. He wasn't really my uncle, although any young kid would have been proud to call him one. Uncle Mac was the retired railroad man who lived next door who tickled me with his wit and his bushy gray mustache. Mac was crippled and walked with a pronounced limp, the result of a catastrophic railroad bridge collapse in which many men had died. Perhaps that was why Uncle Mac valued life so dearly, because he felt so lucky to be alive.

Uncle Mac was good at many things but he especially excelled in catching the gophers that routinely ravaged our lawn. Uncle Mac would set his trusty trap one day and the next morning we'd bow our heads as we laid Mr. Gopher to rest. In his booming voice Uncle Mac would say a few nice words about the gopher and then throw a shovel full of dirt on top the shoe box that was Mr. Gopher's coffin. "Ashes to ashes, dust to dust," Uncle Mac would conclude.

I assure you these gopher funerals were solemn affairs as Uncle Mac was trying to teach us kids the value of life: any life. After the funeral we'd go to his house for a wake, drink cold milk and eat what Uncle Mac called "gopher cookies."

I vividly recall my last gopher funeral at the age of about six. Uncle Mac gave one of his best sermons, once again saying a lot of nice things about Mr. Gopher as if he had known him personally all his life. Then I ruined the solemnity of the occasion by asking: "Uncle Mac, if Mr. Gopher was such a good guy why did you kill him?"

I forgot what Uncle Mac said at the time but many years later I think I've finally figured it out. It wasn't because Mr. Gopher was such an upstanding citizen that we gave him a royal send off. No, it was because Uncle Mac felt guilty about being such a good gopher killer. Those gopher funerals were his conscience calling.

The world today is full of Uncle Macs: People who want their gophers, snakes and cockroaches gone, but can't stand the thought of them being dead. They are the well meaning folks with bumper stickers on the back windows of their cars urging us all to "Save the Monarchs," while their front windshields are splattered with dead bugs and butterflies. They think coyotes are gorgeous as long as they're eating our sheep but something must be done when they kill their free range chickens, cats or park ducks. It depends on whose ox is getting gored, or whose dog is being devoured. Raccoons are cute until they tip over THEIR trash cans. Then they must be evicted from the neighborhood by any means necessary. Mountain lions are fine on our side of the fence but let them sneak on the golf course and it's time to call out the National Guard.

Urbanites routinely exterminate their pests and in lieu of flowers they send donations to green groups. This helps ease their conscience when they hit a deer, call the animal abatement service or step on a snail. They dispatch their guilt by writing a check and promising to feel bad.

City folks are all for relocating wolves and grizzlies just as long as it's not in their backyard. They'll pay lip service to save the prairie dog but not the rats that infest their world. They have hunters in their sights for being uncivilized but they'd blast the deer that eat their flowers with a bazooka if they could get away with it. Our city cousins don't have the foggiest idea how to peacefully coexist with nature but that doesn't stop them from insulting ranchers and country folks who do.

These modern day Uncle Macs stock up at the store on stuff to kill things, like mouse traps, fly swatters, bug bombs, zappers and toxic bait. It eases their conscience to know their traps are padded and their poison fast-acting. They look out on the bleak urban landscape they have created, devoid of animal life, and must feel a little guilty. So they preach sermons, wring their bloody hands and preside over displays of dismay, like undertakers at yet another gopher funeral.

A Farm Family Reunion

I HAVEN'T BEEN to a good old farm family reunion in many a moon. You know the kind, where everybody gets together to see who is falling apart. I'm sure you can remember at least one aunt who left bright red lipstick on your cheek, pinched it and said, "I haven't seen you since you were in dirty diapers?" At family reunions you met in-laws and outlaws you never knew you had, distant relatives you wish would have stayed that way, and cousins once removed you wish someone would have. Removed, that is.

Back when there was still a lot of country in this country nearly everyone was related to someone who still lived on a farm or ranch. That was usually where the family reunion was held. All the branches of the family tree showed up, including those who should have been pruned off long ago. Even the uncle who was a lawyer and the brother-in-law who worked for the IRS were invited, because all the relatives were close... in more than miles. Attendance was high amongst family members because they knew if they didn't show up they'd be the main topic of conversation.

At an old fashioned farm family reunion the fun was home-made and so was the food. You didn't worry about dying from digesting the potato salad, the greens came from a garden and the burgers weren't soy based. It took twenty men around a barbecue pit to decide when the meat was ready. Over hot stoves and tablecloths the women traded recipes and baby pictures. The main meal was served outside, with tables and folding chairs borrowed from the church. There were five kinds of pie served under mounds of fresh whipped cream. At a family reunion no one was on a diet or afraid of the food. The only preservatives present were the ones keeping Aunt Maude alive.

All the young cousins from the big city learned first hand that milk came from a cow and not a carton. They rode a horse for the first time, picked and shucked an ear of corn, bottle fed a bummer lamb, saw kittens being born, fished in a real creek and made memories that would last a lifetime. During a lazy softball game played in a cow pasture everyone was on the same side... the home team. Old men, long past their glory days, reaffirmed bonds written in blood over checkers or cards. Even the oddball kin, the sap in the family tree, were made to feel part of the family. And at the end of the joyous day, when folks were through celebrating freedom, food and family, to a person they would all say, "Let's do this again."

But we never did.

These days if you wanted to have a family reunion you probably wouldn't be able to find addresses for half the fathers, the mothers couldn't take time off from work and the grandparents would have to wear name tags. To round up all the kids in one place you'd have to hold the reunion at their daycare facility, instead of a relative's farm. Just as well, you probably couldn't find a family farm if you went back ten states and two generations. How could you have a farm family reunion where nothing was home grown or homemade? The food would be as foreign as most of the relatives. The fabric that wove families together is now frayed and faded.

When did our society abandon the family and the farm? And why?

Probably when we became obsessed with acquiring stuff and so focused on ourselves. In search of "a better life" we became upwardly and literally mobile. Kids moved off the farm, marriages split and so did relatives, without leaving a forwarding address. These days the only thing missing in the home is the family.

That is why there is no need to look in your mailbox for an invitation to a farm family reunion. That is too bad, because happiness is relative.

BARKER OR BITER?

ANYONE WHO HAS traveled this country's backroads and dirt roads has been faced with the dilemma of arriving at a destination only to be met by a barking dog. The problem is that you only have about five seconds to determine whether the ferocious beast scratching the paint on your car door is a barker or a biter so you can take the appropriate course of action. After decades of visiting out-of-the-way places I have developed some helpful hints that I hope will help.

You should never reach out your hand to an unknown dog unless you want to be known as Stubby or Lefty for the rest of your life.

The farther from a hospital the greater the chance the dog is rabid.

"Toy" dogs like poodles are not to be played with because they suffer from small dog syndrome. Remember, Lhassa Apso means "OUCH" in French.

Never approach a wolf hybrid with long, foamy bicuspids.

Biting is not a breed thing. The biting gene does not seem to be hereditary, except in the case of Mexican Hairless Chihuahuas who have been known to bite through solid steel. Probably because they are upset about going prematurely bald.

Dogs often work in teams. If you see a peaceful Pointer don't get out of your car. He is probably just POINTING you out for the Rottweiller lurking in the bushes.

Animal behaviorists suggest that you can distract a biting dog by throwing an object past its face, triggering the chase instinct. Please understand that this is an unproven theory from a PhD who developed it using a computer model.

DO NOT provoke dogs named Chewie or Bones. A dog with the name "Sic Em" imprinted on his studded collar may lack certain social skills.

Go in disguise. Pretend to be a burglar or a peddler and the dog probably won't touch you. DON'T dress as a repairman or a neighbor returning something.

Biting dogs don't follow stereotypes. Chow Chows don't always live up to their name and some Dobermen's bark is worse than their bite. On the other hand, that harmless looking Dachshund eying your leg may want to satisfy its daily nutritional needs by dining on formerly attached human body parts.

Biters are like team ropers...they are either headers or heelers. To confuse them stand like a mummy with your chin and all appendages tucked into your body.

To reduce the risk of injury, stock your vehicle with protective devices such as pepper spray, hot shots, mace, guns, baseball bats and a dozen donuts for off duty Police Dogs with brutality on their minds.

If you are attacked by a "biter" take a page from the dog's bag of tricks by rolling over and playing dead.

Haul your own dog in the back of your vehicle and if it refuses to get out of the truck, do likewise.

Read body language. The best indication that a dog is a biter is if the hair stands up on the back of the neck. Your neck, not the dogs.

The most dangerous dog is not a barker or a biter but one bearing a slobbery tennis ball or other retrievable object in its mouth. NEVER show any friendly intentions toward such an animal! This mongrel will not bite because it ALWAYS has the ball in its mouth. The danger is that in a moment of weakness you will throw the ball and be forced to continue hurling the object until the mutt dies of old age.

THE PETTING ZOO

I HAVE ALWAYS loved animals and when I was little I constantly pestered my parents to take me to the zoo. My mom always sarcastically replied, "When they want you they'll come and get you."

I guess I was kind of a terror as a kid. My mom's only hope was that I'd either grow up fast or run away from home. But when I grew up all I ever wanted to be was a kid. I never dreamed about running away to join the circus but I did dream about running away with the petting zoo.

My fellow juvenile delinquents and I called the nice fellow who ran the petting zoo "The Animal Man." He had a little farm on the outskirts of town and whenever anyone asked him he'd load up his old pickup and dilapidated horse trailer with his menagerie and bring the petting zoo to town. He'd set up in front of the grocery store on a Saturday afternoon to help the Girl Scouts sell cookies or the Methodist Church to sell raffle tickets. He and his animals were always present at the festival that every small town in our county staged to celebrate their particular claim to fame. Whether it was the Lemon Festival or the Strawberry Carnival you could count on the Animal Man to be there.

Admission to the petting zoo was free of charge but if you wanted to feed the chickens, ducks or geese the Animal Man would sell you a little sack of feed for a dime. I suppose he supplemented his meager income by selling those little sacks of grain. I'll never forget the time we brought our own feed. I think it was about the funniest thing I ever saw watching that sow try to eat the giant sized Tootsie Roll® we fed it.

Some of his animals could even do tricks. The dog welcomed each guest by shaking their paw and the Animal Man had rigged up a Ferris wheel for the baby chicks.

Bales of hay protected the ducks from the goats, but from the people there was no protection. The petting zoo was always noisy with barnyard sounds, not so much from the animals but from the parents who were always asking their kids, "Now what sound does the goose make?" Then a whole gaggle of parents would go "honk, honk, honk." It was almost as funny as watching the parents squirm and sweat when their kids asked how baby animals are made.

The petting zoo gave our parents a chance to show us how smart and worldly they were. If by chance someone in the crowd had actually milked a cow once that was enough to make that person a local celebrity. The grown-ups knew important things too, like the fact that the male of the species is always the prettiest, that goats eat tin cans and that if you held a chick you could get chicken pox. Despite the   poor quality of information being dispensed, the Animal Man never said a word. He would just smile and fill the camera frame full of family as we all gathered around a baby calf for a scrapbook picture.

The Animal Man doesn't bring the petting zoo to town any more. The liability insurance got too high, even though about the worst thing I ever saw happen was a little chick pooped in the mayor's hand at the Lemon Festival once. I suppose it's no big deal, after all, it was just a dumb petting zoo.

Occasionally the Animal Man is spotted downtown shuffling along and two generations of parents will reflect on those glorious days when we first discovered the wonders of the animal world. Those parents bring their kids up to meet and to touch the Animal Man now, as if he himself was in some kind of a petting zoo. Sadly, for some kids, that is as close as they'll ever get.

THE DAY YOUR DOG DIES

S HE WAS THE ONLY dog in my life I actually paid money for and yet she was about the most useless. I can remember the day we got her like it was yesterday. I only wish it was, maybe then I could have prevented her death.

To the Working Kelpie Council of Australia her name was Ballydine Patriece but we just called her Aussie. We picked her out before she opened her eyes at the Ballydine Kelpie Stud, Uralla, New South Wales, Australia. I suppose I always resented the fact that Aussie visited Hawaii before I ever did but that is where she spent her quarantine period. Aussie came to our country as a reluctant guest. When she arrived in San Francisco she took one step out of the wire cage on to the slippery floor, fell on her belly, sprawled out on all four puppy paws and immediately tried to get back into her cage.

Aussie had some real famous parents you probably never heard of and I had visions of becoming a dog trainer. So we tried to get her bred and make a lot of money off her reproductive parts. Knowing this, Aussie refused to conceive. She was supposed to be a working dog, but in retrospect I think she came from a non-working strain. In fact, as I look back now Aussie had several bad habits. She refused to ride in the back of the truck preferring instead the comfort of the cab. When we worked cattle we had to lock her in the house and when we worked sheep there were times we unexpectedly ate mutton for dinner. Aussie caused us several sleepless nights, usually by barking at intruders that existed only in her canine mind. Then there was the night she spent in the pound after running away. And boy did she cost us money. Her football knee operation alone cost $225.

But if Aussie was not the perfect dog neither were we perfect pet parents. We never gave her a birthday present or sent her to obedience school. My wife never knitted her a sweater or made her homemade doggie biscuits. And I suppose there were rare occasions when we argued in front of her. But that was only natural, Aussie was our one and only child.

Aussie was a member of our family. If you'll pardon the parental pride I could brag that Aussie was loyal, good looking and funny. She was the source of several stories and I never had to pay her royalties. She kept my wife company when I was gone and my wife insists she was much better company. A better listener for sure. Aussie hardly ever got sick and had no really disgusting habits. She had a strong eye, a big heart and was always glad to see us.

I suppose that's why I cried the day she died.

It was my fault too. For 14 years I had cared for her carefully but on this day I got too engrossed in a project on the ranch and I suppose

Aussie felt a little ignored. Either that or perhaps she finally got the urge to meet a male dog after fourteen years. But 14 years to a dog is 98 in people years so I really doubt it. Whatever it was that made her stray she ran on to the road that borders our place and you can imagine what happened next. Cars are the curse of dogs. I bet up in doggie heaven they cuss the name of Henry Ford.

This dog had meant more to me than most humans but we didn't dress up in suits or have a funeral procession. No, Aussie didn't even get mentioned in a newspaper obituary. I suppose I could rationalize her death by saying that she was getting old anyway, and that she did die immediately, but somehow that doesn't help.

Now every time I pass that fatal spot on the road or pass a telephone pole with a poster for a missing dog I think of Aussie and the pain that others feel when their dog dies. They say that the best thing to do is to get another dog right away. But I don't buy it. In fact, right now I don't think I ever want another dog. I'm not so sure all the joy Aussie brought us during her life was worth the pain I felt the day she died.

Rules We Forgot

I AM REMINDED on a daily basis that most people in this country have either forgotten or are not paying any attention to the basic rules of our society. If this applies to you I'd like to refresh your memory.

Slow traffic should drive in the slow lane. That's why it's called the SLOW lane.

When the National Anthem is being sung at a ball game please take your hat off your head and place it over your heart. And just because you don't know the words to the song does not mean it's time to talk or swill beer.

Speak softly and carry a big stick. Please note, the rule is NOT speak loudly and carry a small phone. While we're on the subject of cell phones: Please keep your voice down. If I wanted to know all about your pathetic life I would have kept my party line.

At a four-way stop if two cars arrive at the same time the vehicle to the right has the right of way, not the car with the loudest stereo or the biggest rims.

Your mother specifically said to wear good underwear when going out in case you got in an accident. She did NOT mean we wanted to see the underwear of teenage boys with baggy pants three sizes too large.

Remember sidewalks? They are for pedestrians and are not the exclusive domain of skateboarders, bicyclers and panhandlers.

Dirty words are still dirty. If you use such language please don't do it in front of my wife. It embarrasses all of us.

Don't hit. Even if you think you can get away with it or suspect the other person will get penalized for striking back. Life is not a Monday night NFL game.

If the sign at the grocery store says a maximum of 15 items they are referring to you too, as hard as that may be to believe.

Majority rules. This means we don't have to pander to the whims of a bunch of liberal bed wetting chuckleheads or constantly apologize to victims rights groups.

There have been no major rule changes; the magic words are still please, thank you and excuse me.

Eat your vegetables and don't bite the hand that feeds you. This means we shouldn't be taking away water rights from farmers or ranchers or pass stupid regulations that make their job any harder than it already is.

Gentlemen still open doors for ladies. If you don't you are either saying she's not a lady or you are not a gentleman. And it is still impolite to telephone during dinner. If you are a telemarketer it is impolite to call between the hours of January through December.

If there are five cars behind you please pull over. Although you may be retired and on permanent vacation in your oversized RV that does not mean the rest of us want to smell your exhaust or travel across country at thirty-five miles per hour.

You are guaranteed life, liberty and the pursuit of happiness in this country. This doesn't mean you can do anything you want just because you have a high-priced attorney and good insurance.

Children are to be seen and not heard. If I am interrupted one more time by a bratty child in mid-sentence I swear I'm going to count to three.

There are still only Ten Commandments. They have not been amended or revised and God still does not grade on a curve.

ONE HORSE POWER

THE WORLD STARTED going down hill the day we parked the horse. If we had only stuck with the horse we would not have drunk drivers, car recalls, finance companies or automobile insurance. Terms such as parts and labor, optional equipment and self-serve would never have become part of our vocabulary.

Oh, I suppose the horse did at times become a pain in the behind, but trading up to a contraption known to the western movie goer as the "buckboard" created a problem we men folk still must contend with. The buckboard had a front seat big enough for the wife to sit next to her husband. This made it possible for the wife to bark out instructions such as, "Shouldn't we be going a little faster? Slow down! Watch that turn!"

The first cowboys soon tired of having just one horse per person so they added a few more horses so they could pull a bigger wagon known as the stage coach. This allowed the cowboys to put their wives in the back seat, thus creating the very first back seat drivers.

But the speeds reached by the six horse hitches did not make the grade, so those early pioneers created machines with the power of 350 horses. They named these contraptions after the horses they replaced, names like Pintos and Mavericks. The new Mustang had many advertised advantages over the old equine model. For instance, you could listen to a tape deck while you waited in a gas line or a traffic jam.

In the days of one horse power the only pollution on city streets was caused by a horse that had been eating too many legumes. But the automobile, with the power of hundreds of horses, has made it possible to blanket entire cities in smog. Try cleaning that up with a shovel!

Replacing horses with automobiles also made it possible for a once strong country to become dependent on Arab oil sheiks, who by the way, still ride camels. The big cars made in Detroit grew out of fashion because they cost too much to feed so the blacktop cowboys began buying foreign cars, which then made it possible for a once strong economy to become dependent on Japan.

A good horse in the old days cost about fifty bucks. Add optional equipment such as a saddle and a bridle and you might have had a hundred dollars invested in some pretty reliable transportation. The new cars are a little more expensive and a lot less reliable. My horse, Gentleman, lived to a grand old age of 25 years but my truck died at the age of four. If my truck was a horse at least I could shoot it to put it out of its misery. The engine won't start and the payments won't stop. And once a month I get a good case of car sickness, when the payment comes due. I am told, however, that I can get back on my feet if I just miss a couple payments.

Man has always wanted to go faster, faster, faster. So he invented subways, busses and that other form of the traveling slum, the airplane. The airplane allows 400 people to travel with the speed of a thousand horses and to all watch a bad movie at the same time. The airplane is the ultimate in speed as long as you remember to order your ticket a year in advance and don't care if you stay over a Saturday night. Otherwise you can't afford to go. And prices are going up as more planes are coming down. At least a horse can't fall thirty thousand feet!

I think I liked horsepower better when only horses had it.

THE HORSE AND THE HUMMINGBIRD

IF I COULD BE anything other than what I am, a lowly writer and cow poke, I'd like to be a veterinarian. Not because of the low pay, long hours, strange people and sick animals you meet. It's just that all the vets I've ever met have been such kind and caring people. They are the kind of good folks that you'd enjoy having over for dinner if they wouldn't charge you for the house call.

I dropped by our local vet clinic the other day to pick up some supplies. Usually it is quite a zany place with a menagerie of animals waiting to be treated, but this day was not as jovial as most. A white horse with a twisted gut was tied to a post trembling in pain. The sleepy vet had stayed up all night trying to straighten things out but one look at the horse was proof the attempt had been in vain.

I listened as Dr. Don called the horse's owner to explain that he had done everything possible to save the horse but there was no alternative but to put the horse down. From what I heard of the one-sided conversation it sounded like they both agreed it was the merciful thing to do. Both the good Doctor and the horse had suffered enough. As I watched the Doc inject the drug that would end the horse's suffering I realized that being a veterinarian certainly had its downside. Dr. Don told me no matter how many times he had put an animal out of its misery, it still hurt him inside.

While the Doc was putting the horse down an unexpected visitor came into the clinic. An adolescent and wayward hummingbird flew in the door and up to the skylight, thinking it was the way out. It was beating its tiny body against the plastic window in an attempt to vacate the premises.

Before I realized what was happening Doctor Don was climbing up a ladder on the outside of the building. At first I was a little miffed because I had been waiting for awhile. But I calmed down when I realized what the Doc was up to. After getting on the roof Dr. Don slipped and slid on the shake roof over to where the skylight was. Then he placed a heavy blanket over the skylight so that the hummingbird would not think it was the way out. Unfortunately it didn't work.

I grew up under the mistaken belief that a hummingbird's wings are always in constant motion. But this hummingbird's wings had stopped fluttering. I didn't know if the tiny bird had given up or was just ensnared in the cobwebs that covered the ceiling of the vet clinic. At any rate, the hummingbird was no longer beating itself against the skylight. Perhaps it had joined the horse, their last flight skyward. But the vet did not give up that easily, after all, this was a man who had just stayed up all night in a near hopeless attempt to save a horse. Why not a hummingbird?

The next thing I knew he had brought the ladder inside the building and was climbing towards the skylight with conviction. It seemed to this observer that the loss of the horse had made this mercy mission all the more important. As he climbed the ladder he apologized for delaying his attention from my mundane matters but actually, I didn't mind waiting. Trying to help, I steadied the ladder as the Doc reached up as high as he possibly could. In his big, highly trained hand he grasped the tiny bird cloaked in cobwebs. I was sure the bird was dead. The most amazing thing happened next. Carefully Dr. Don removed most of the cobwebs that held the hummingbird captive. Then he walked outside, closing the door to the clinic and placed the tiny bird on the ground. To my amazement the tiny wings began to flutter and the hummingbird took flight.

The box score of Dr. Don's performance that day might read: won one, lost one. The good doc was batting .500. The vet had saved the patient with no owner to pay a bill or show appreciation. He had saved the patient that couldn't pay in cash and lost the paying customer. He saved a hummingbird and lost a $3,000 horse. But I have a feeling in the eyes of God and my vet, that day there was no difference between a horse and a hummingbird.

COMMENCE

DEAR NEPHEW,

Rather than buy you the traditional gold pen for your graduation I thought I'd retrieve the one I received 35 years ago and write you a letter. I never write with the valuable pen, it just sits in its velvet lined box never getting used. In that respect it's like much of what you have just learned in school. On the occasion of your graduation I'd like to tell you some things I wish someone would have told me.

It is traditional at commencement to tell graduates that the world is a stage just waiting for their appearance. I'm sorry to inform you that the world couldn't care less about your graduation. Tomorrow you become just another person to be taxed, harassed, worked to death, borrowed from and promised to.

There will be people who are not impressed with your fancy diploma or your expensive education because they have neither. Play it down. In your first job you will be under-utilized and little appreciated. Your boss will not be as smart or as energetic as you but that doesn't mean you'll soon take over his corner office. That's the system. Don't fight it, you won't change a thing. Just remember that when you are old (in your forties) the same system will protect your job at that point in your life when you are trying to put your kids through college.

As you begin your career be advised that loyalty is more important than intelligence. At first you will not get paid what you are worth but at the other end of your career you'll be paid far more than you earn. Nobody owes you a job and before you quit the one you have, be sure to have some place else to go. Or, if you think it's so easy...mind your own business. The world finds room for entrepreneurs.

Choosing a mate will be the most important decision you'll ever make. Rather than selecting one on looks alone you might as well pick someone that you don't like and give them half of everything. If you want children make sure it's not just to save your marriage. Get a dog instead. It won't work either but at least you messed up a dog's life and not a child's.

Don't buy an expensive car just to distinguish yourself from people of lesser status. And remember, a car will last longer than its 48 month mortgage. Drive an older car and save the money. Throw your credit cards away and never pay more for fancy labels when a cheaper brand will do just fine.

Don't worry too much about how you look. Fretting over how you arrange the hairs on your head will cause you to lose them. Your fellow employees will care far more about your punctuality than the width of the lapels on your suit.

To live a long life avoid dying. This is best accomplished by having hobbies. Rather than watching TV take long walks, read books or listen to good music. Stay active by playing sports instead of just watching them. If you don't have time to mow your own lawn or clean your own house you are much too busy. In business and in life take chances but not short cuts. When you get lost ask directions. Keep in touch with family and don't have too many good friends. Don't ever buy anything over the phone from someone you don't know and always read the small print.

Take vacations and keep scrapbooks to remind you of the good times. Smell the roses while your sense of smell still works. Don't drink and drive. One incident can ruin your whole life and maybe that of another.

Don't lose much sleep over global war or warming. Just make sure you recycle, be a good neighbor and vote. You are NOT your brother's keeper. And just because you graduated from college do not ever use it as an excuse to stop learning.

So what's stopping you... commence.

ABOUT THE AUTHOR

LEE PITTS IS THE executive editor for Livestock Market Digest, a newspaper serving the livestock industry. He is the author of seven previous books and a syndicated weekly humor column. His is a recognized byline in rural weekly newspapers and monthly magazines throughout the country. When not traveling down dirt roads in search of stories he makes his home in Los Osos, California, with his wife, Diane.

ABOUT THE ARTIST

TIM COX IS ONE of the best known western artists in America. His depiction of the contemporary cowboy, rancher and the modern West has made him a favorite of collectors and connoisseurs of western art. Tim is a three time winner of the Museum Purchase Award at Cheyenne Frontier Days and his paintings have graced the covers of countless magazines. He resides with his wife, Suzie, and their children in Bloomfield, New Mexico. Tim can be reached at 505/632-8080 or through his web site: www.timcox.com.

If you enjoyed this collection of essays please check your local bookstore for these books by Lee Pitts, or order directly from us.

People Who Live At The End of Dirt Roads

Featuring essays heard on Paul Harvey and reprinted in Chicken Soup for the Golden Soul. Includes These Things I Wish and People Who Live At The End of Dirt Roads. Illustrated by Don Dane. $10.95

Back Door People

More heartwarming and humorous adventures selected from the best of Lee's syndicated column. Contains many of Lee's favorite animal stories. Illustrated by Vel Miller. $11.95

Essays From God's Country

If you are from the country, or merely one of many who would like to be, you are sure to enjoy this collection of highly requested essays from Lee Pitts. Cover by Tim Cox. $12.95

Please add $2.00 per book for postage and handling. California residents add 7.25% sales tax. Make checks payable to Lee Pitts and mail to: P.O. Box 616, Morro Bay, CA 93443.